Rookie Read-About® Geography

# Louisiana

## By Judith Jensen Hyde

**Subject Consultant**
Greg Lambousy
Director of Collections
Louisiana State Museum
New Orleans, Louisiana

**Reading Consultant**
Cecilia Minden-Cupp, PhD
Former Director of the Language and Literacy Program
Harvard Graduate School of Education
Cambridge, Massachusetts

Children's Press ®
A Division of Scholastic Inc.
New York   Toronto   London   Auckland   Sydney
Mexico City   New Delhi   Hong Kong
Danbury, Connecticut

Designer: Herman Adler
Photo Researcher: Caroline Anderson
The photo on the cover shows a swamp in Louisiana.

**Library of Congress Cataloging-in-Publication Data**

Hyde, Judith Jensen, 1947–
    Louisiana / by Judith Jensen Hyde.
        p. cm. — (Rookie read-about geography)
    Includes index.
    ISBN 13: 978-0-516-21848-9 (lib. bdg.)        978-0-516-21747-5 (pbk.)
    ISBN 10: 0-516-21848-4 (lib. bdg.)              0-516-21747-X (pbk.)
    1. Louisiana—Juvenile literature. I. Title. II. Series.
    F369.3.H94 2007
    976.3—dc22                                               2006007154

What has a big mouth, sharp teeth, and lives in Louisiana? An alligator! The alligator is Louisiana's state reptile.

Louisiana is in the southern United States. It touches Texas, Arkansas, Mississippi, and the Gulf of Mexico.

Can you find Louisiana on this map?

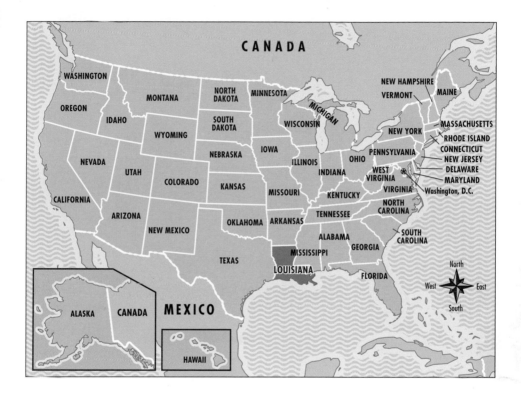

CANADA

WASHINGTON

OREGON

IDAHO

MONTANA

NORTH DAKOTA

MINNESOTA

MICHIGAN

WISCONSIN

WYOMING

SOUTH DAKOTA

NEVADA

UTAH

NEBRASKA

IOWA

ILLINOIS

INDIANA

OHIO

PENNSYLVANIA

NEW YORK

NEW HAMPSHIRE

VERMONT

MAINE

MASSACHUSETTS

RHODE ISLAND

CONNECTICUT

NEW JERSEY

DELAWARE

MARYLAND

CALIFORNIA

COLORADO

KANSAS

MISSOURI

KENTUCKY

WEST VIRGINIA

VIRGINIA

Washington, D.C.

ARIZONA

NEW MEXICO

OKLAHOMA

ARKANSAS

TENNESSEE

NORTH CAROLINA

SOUTH CAROLINA

TEXAS

ALABAMA

MISSISSIPPI

LOUISIANA

GEORGIA

FLORIDA

North

West        East

South

ALASKA

CANADA

MEXICO

HAWAII

5

A swamp on the West Gulf Coastal Plain

Louisiana is divided into three sections, or regions. These are the East Gulf Coastal Plain, the Mississippi Alluvial (al-LU-vee-uhl) Plain, and the West Gulf Coastal Plain.

The East Gulf Coastal Plain is east of the Mississippi River.

Lousiana black bears and salamanders live in this area.

A salamander

Lake Pontchartrain

The East Gulf Coastal
Plain lies just north
of Lake Pontchartrain
(LAYK PAHNT-shar-trayn).
This is the largest lake
in Louisiana.

The Mississippi Alluvial Plain runs along the Mississippi River from Arkansas to the Gulf of Mexico.

This region is filled with forests, swamps, and lakes.

A swamp on the Mississippi Alluvial Plain

A nutria

The Mississippi Delta formed where the Mississippi River meets the Gulf of Mexico. A delta is sand and soil that collect where a river empties into a larger body of water.

Swamp rabbits and animals called nutria (NU-tree-uh) live in the delta.

The West Gulf Coastal Plain is in western Louisiana.

This region is filled with prairies, hills, and marshes. Marshes are areas of soft, wet, grassy land.

A marsh on the West Gulf Coastal Plain

A Louisiana bayou

Slow-moving streams called bayous (BYE-yooz) flow through marshes in the southern part of the West Gulf Coastal Plain.

Low sandy ridges called cheniers (shuh-NEARS) separate marshes from the gulf.

Baton Rouge (BAHT-uhn RUZH) is the capital of Louisiana and is its largest city.

New Orleans is another famous city in Louisiana. It is famous for its jazz music.

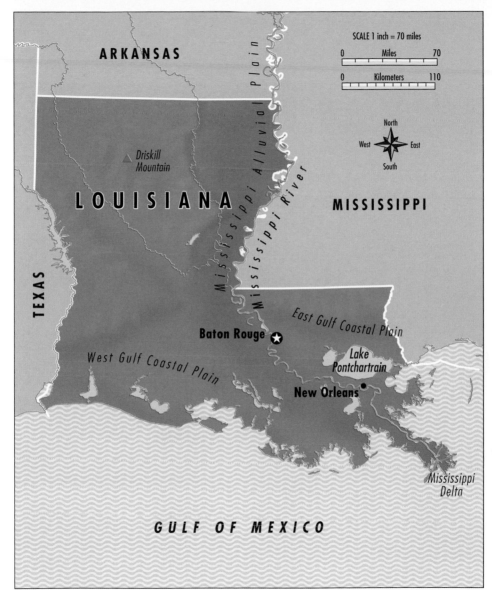

SCALE 1 inch = 70 miles

| 0 | Miles | 70 |

| 0 | Kilometers | 110 |

ARKANSAS

Mississippi Alluvial Plain

North

West East

South

Driskill
Mountain

LOUISIANA

MISSISSIPPI

Mississippi River

TEXAS

East Gulf Coastal Plain

Baton Rouge ★

Lake
Pontchartrain

West Gulf Coastal Plain

New Orleans

Mississippi
Delta

GULF OF MEXICO

21

Flooding in New Orleans in 2005

Much of New Orleans flooded when Hurricane Katrina hit Louisiana in 2005. A hurricane is a storm with strong, destructive winds.

People in Louisiana are working hard to rebuild their state.

Farmers in Louisiana grow cotton and sugarcane plants. The sugar in your home comes from sugarcane.

Louisiana fishers catch shrimp, crabs, and crawfish. Crawfish look like little lobsters.

Other Louisiana products include oil and gas.

A Louisiana fisher catches crawfish.

An eastern brown pelican

Louisiana is home to many animals. Alligators, snakes, and raccoons live here.

Birds often build nests near the water. Louisiana's state bird is the eastern brown pelican.

Maybe one day you'll
visit Louisiana!

What will you do first
when you get there?

A family canoes through a Louisiana swamp.

# Words You Know

alligator

bayou

crawfish

eastern brown pelican

30

Lake Pontchartrain

marsh

nutria

salamander

31

# Index

## About the Author

For the past several years, Judith Jensen Hyde has worked as a graphic artist and a television technician for a large school district in the Kansas City area. Judith and her husband have one grown daughter, a dog, a cat, and a grand-cat.

## Photo Credits